HIP-HOP

Notorious B.I.G.

Hal Marcovitz

Mason Crest Publishers

Notorious B.I.G.

FRONTIS Christopher Wallace (1972–1997), who performed under the name
Notorious B.I.G., was a talented rapper whose brief career had a great
influence on hip-hop music.

PRODUCED BY 21ST CENTURY PUBLISHING AND COMMUNICATIONS, INC.

MASON CREST PUBLISHERS INC.
370 Reed Road
Broomall, Pennsylvania 19008
(866)MCP-BOOK (toll free)
www.masoncrest.com

Printed in Malaysia.

9 8 7 6 5 4 3 2

Library of Congress Cataloging-in-Publication Data

Marcovitz, Hal.
   Notorious B.I.G. / Hal Marcovitz.
      p. cm. — (Hip-hop)
   Includes bibliographical references (p.   ) and index.
ISBN-13: 978-1-4222-0124-4 (hc)
ISBN-10: 1-4222-0124-4 (hc)
   1. Notorious B.I.G. (Musician)—Juvenile literature. 2. Rapmusicians—United
States—Biography—Juvenile literature. I. Title.II. Series.
ML3930.N68M37 2006
782.421649092—dc22
[B]   2006011441

Publisher's notes:
- All quotations in this book come from original sources, and contain the spelling
  and grammatical inconsistencies of the original text.

- The Web sites mentioned in this book were active at the time of publication.
  The publisher is not responsible for Web sites that have changed their addresses
  or discontinued operation since the date of publication. The publisher will review
  and update the Web site addresses each time the book is reprinted.

Contents

Hip-Hop Timeline

1974 Hip-hop pioneer Afrika Bambaataa organizes the Universal Zulu Nation.

1988 *Yo! MTV Raps* premieres on MTV.

1970s Hip-hop as a cultural movement begins in the Bronx, New York City.

1985 *Krush Groove*, a hip-hop film about Def Jam Recordings, is released featuring Run-D.M.C., Kurtis Blow, LL Cool J, and the Beastie Boys.

1970s DJ Kool Herc pioneers the use of breaks, isolations, and repeats using two turntables.

1979 The Sugarhill Gang's song "Rapper's Delight" is the first hip-hop single to go gold.

1986 Run-D.M.C. are the first rappers to appear on the cover of *Rolling Stone* magazine.

1970   **1980**   **1988**

1976 Grandmaster Flash & the Furious Five pioneer hip-hop MCing and freestyle battles.

1986 Beastie Boys' album *Licensed to Ill* is released and becomes the best-selling rap album of the 1980s.

1970s Break dancing emerges at parties and in public places in New York City.

1982 Afrika Bambaataa embarks on the first European hip-hop tour.

1970s Graffiti artist Vic pioneers tagging on subway trains in New York City.

1988 Hip-hop music annual record sales reaches $100 million.

1984 *Graffiti Rock*, the first hip-hop television program, premieres.

1993 Rapper Snoop Dogg's album *Doggystyle* is the first debut album to hit the music charts at number one.

2006 Queen Latifah becomes the first hip-hop artist to receive a star on the Hollywood Walk of Fame.

1989 DJ Jazzy Jeff & The Fresh Prince become the first hip-hop artists to win a Grammy Award.

2003 Rapper Eminem becomes the first hip-hop artist to win an Academy Award.

2005 Hip-hop artist Kanye West appears on the cover of *Time* magazine.

1989 Rap is added as a new category to the *Billboard* charts.

1997 East Coast rapper Notorious B.I.G. (aka Biggie Smalls) is murdered.

2004 First National Hip-Hop Political Convention is held in Newark, New Jersey.

1989   **2000**   **2006**

1990s Hip-hop emerges in Europe.

1996 West Coast rapper Tupac Shakur is shot and killed.

2005 Rapper Will Smith opens the Philadelphia Live 8 concert as part of 10 simultaneous concerts held worldwide to bring attention to the extreme poverty in Africa.

1989 First gangsta rap album, *Straight Outta Compton*, is released by N.W.A.

2001 The hip-hop political action group, Hip-Hop Summit Action Network, is founded by Russell Simmons.

2006 The Smithsonian Institute National Museum of American History announces the creation of a new hip-hop exhibition scheduled to open in three to five years.

1992 Dr. Dre's album *The Chronic* is released; it redefines West Coast rap.

Notorious B.I.G., also known as Biggie Smalls, receives awards for his debut album, *Ready to Die*, at a 1995 ceremony. Although his career was booming, Biggie had been drawn into the bitter rivalry between his friend Sean "Puffy" Combs and West Coast rap mogul Marion "Suge" Knight.

1

Triumph Turns Sour

The *Source* magazine's nationally televised Second Annual Hip-Hop Awards ceremony should have been an evening of triumph for the rapper Biggie Smalls. Recording under the name Notorious B.I.G., he scored four major awards in the competition, even though he had burst onto the hip-hop scene just a few months before.

On August 3, 1995, the evening of the show, Biggie walked onto the stage at the Paramount Theater in New York City to claim his awards. He was named New Artist of the Year, Lyricist of the Year, and Live Performer of the Year. In addition, he won Album of the Year for *Ready to Die*, which had hit the top of the hip-hop charts soon after its release.

Notorious B.I.G.'s moment in the spotlight was soon lost, though. Leaders of the West Coast hip-hop movement leveled insults from the stage at Biggie's New York–based record label, Bad Boy Entertainment. Bad feelings between Marion "Suge" Knight, head of Death Row Records in

Los Angeles, and Sean "Puffy" Combs of Bad Boy had been building for months.

Tempers Ignite

Knight and Combs had once been friendly rivals. Soon after the two had launched their labels, they occasionally visited each other, sharing insights about the record industry and discussing strategies for building their companies. And Biggie Smalls had once had a friend at Death Row Records. Tupac Shakur, who had become Knight's biggest star, was originally from New York. As the two men had climbed to the top of the hip-hot charts, their paths had often crossed. Shakur had become a star first but had not forgotten Biggie. One night, Shakur had spotted Biggie in the audience at a club where he was performing, and invited him onto the stage with him.

The relationship between the East Coast and West Coast rappers and their producers had started going sour by 1994. Suge Knight bristled at Bad Boy's music, claiming it was a poor imitation of the gritty "gangsta" sound that had become a hallmark of Death Row Records. So when Knight walked on stage at the Paramount Theater to accept an award for Death Row, his anger about Bad Boy's music had been building. In his comments, he directly insulted Combs. "Any artist out there that want to be an artist and want to stay a star and don't want to worry about the executive producer all up in the videos, all on the records—dancing, come to Death Row!" he declared, according to Cheo Coker's biography of Biggie, *Unbelievable*.

Other Death Row rappers, including Snoop Dogg, leveled similar insults from the stage. Said Snoop, according to Coker, "The East Coast ain't got no love for Dr. Dre and Snoop Doggy Dogg? And Death Row? *Y'all don't love us!?* Then let it be known that we got no love for the East Coast then!"

Combs followed Knight and others on stage to present an award to Snoop. When it was his turn to speak, according to Coker, Combs tried to make peace:

"Contrary to what other people may feel, I'm proud of Dr. Dre and Death Row and Suge Knight for their accomplishments. I'm a positive black man, and I want to bring us together, not separate us. All this East and West, that need to stop. One love!"

Rappers Tupac Shakur (left) and Snoop Dogg (center) pose for a promotional picture with Suge Knight, head of Death Row Records. Knight's reputation as a dangerous man who surrounded himself with thugs and convicts gave the label credibility among fans of gangsta rap.

Still, tempers remained hot. Following the awards ceremony, the two sides encountered each other outside the theater. A dispute took place. In the midst of the confrontation, one of Biggie's bodyguards reportedly took out a gun.

Talk It Out?

The comments made that night exposed a growing hostility that the press would soon label the "East Coast–West Coast Rap War." Just a few weeks after the awards show, famed music producer Quincy Jones tried to settle the feud. He called Knight and Combs together to air

Puffy Combs and Notorious B.I.G. perform together during a concert. Though Combs was a talented and successful rap producer, Knight and others at Death Row made fun of Puffy's habit of joining his artists on stage or appearing in their music videos.

their complaints. Snoop Dogg, Dr. Dre, and Biggie Smalls also sat in on the meeting.

Mostly Jones hoped to remind those gathered that music should be a positive force in society; he also wanted them to stop threatening each other. To reinforce his message, Jones invited several leaders of the African-American community to speak at the meeting. Among the speakers who attended this hip-hop **summit** were Colin Powell, a military leader and diplomat who would later be appointed U.S. Secretary of State; and Minister Conrad Muhammad, a leader of the religious sect Nation of Islam. "Speaker after speaker talked about power as a form of responsibility," Jones later wrote, "about being guided by the inner conscience, even if anger is the initial motivator for your actions." However, the meeting failed to defuse the anger and hostility that had been building for months. When the rappers left the hotel, nothing had been settled.

Despite the trouble, Biggie Smalls told reporters that he was not worried about the escalating violence of the rivalry between Death Row and Bad Boy. "I'll be the cool dude," he told reporters. "I have security, and they can handle that. I'm just the cool dude. Write the raps, do the shows, all that."

In reality, Notorious B.I.G. did have reason to be concerned about the rap war. Biggie Smalls had gained fame rapping about life on the **urban** streets, which he portrayed as dominated by murder, robbery, and other violent crimes. As Biggie and other gangsta rappers who had grown up in tough neighborhoods knew too well, it was a way of life they often found impossible to leave behind.

Growing up in a poor Brooklyn neighborhood, Christopher Wallace stood out because of his size. As a teenager, he was more than six feet tall and weighed over 300 pounds. He also stood out because of his talent as an amateur rapper.

2

Big Chris

Christopher Wallace, the future Notorious B.I.G., was born May 21, 1972, in the Clinton Hill neighborhood of Brooklyn, New York. Clinton Hill is a racially mixed, working-class neighborhood with its share of drug and crime problems. Chris hoped to rise above the poverty of his neighborhood by making a name for himself as a rapper.

Chris's mother, Voletta Wallace, had emigrated to the United States from Jamaica, moving to an apartment in Clinton Hill just before her son was born. Soon after Chris's birth, Voletta and Chris's father, George Latore, divorced. Voletta, who finished college at night and then worked as a teacher, provided her son with a good home and instilled a work ethic in him. By the time Chris was 11, he was already earning money at a food market. He was an excellent student, an accomplished artist, and hoped to go to college to study commercial art.

Chris and his friends enjoyed rapping—chanting rhymes to a fast-paced beat. During the 1980s, when Chris was a young boy, rap was just starting to dominate the music industry. Many of the kids in Chris's Brooklyn neighborhood were amateur rappers, but Chris was truly dedicated to the music and known for constantly making up rhymes. He told friends he wanted to be a famous rapper.

Chris was also well known around the neighborhood for another reason—he grew into a very tall and very large young man. By the time he hit his teens, Chris stood six feet two inches tall and weighed more than three hundred pounds. Around the neighborhood, he was known as "Big Chris."

Chris often found himself in minor scrapes with the law. Usually his run-ins with police would entail his being taken down to the local precinct headquarters where he was questioned and then released. Chris was sensitive and often broke into tears as he waited in the station house for his mother to come. Detective Andre Parker told Cathy Scott, author of *The Murder of Biggie Smalls*, "Yeah, he'd have a fit when we brought him in. He'd cry and say, 'I ain't doin' nothin'. I swear it.' He was just this chunky kid. A scared kid." Often, while choking back the tears, Chris would tell the detectives, "I'm gonna be famous one day. You wait 'n see. I'm gonna be *big*."

"That Is Not Music!"

Voletta constantly pleaded with Chris to stay out of trouble, but she found it difficult to reach her son. By the time he was 14, Chris's teachers were reporting that he had lost interest in his studies and had been skipping many classes. Eventually, police told Voletta that while they were at her apartment building for an investigation, they found Chris's schoolbooks hidden on the roof. He had stopped going to school during the day, but would get the books in the afternoon so that his mother would not know. "I confronted him and it turned uglier and uglier," Voletta wrote in her book about Biggie.

Even as Chris's rebellious attitude grew, he maintained his intense passion for music and rapping. Chris's voice was deep, husky, and harsh—hardly the voice Voletta expected from a recording artist. Voletta did not know anything about rap, though, and therefore did not understand that the beat, the rhymes, and what the rapper has to say are the most important elements of the music.

Christopher's mother, Voletta Wallace, worked as a teacher and hoped her son would get a good education. She did not like or understand rap music, which had just emerged as an art form during the late 1970s, when Chris was a little boy.

BIGGIE

VOLETTA WALLACE REMEMBERS HER SON, CHRISTOPHER WALLACE, AKA NOTORIOUS B.I.G.

Voletta Wallace

with Tre McKenzie

Foreword by Faith Evans

Voletta Wallace has published a book about her son. "Christopher was a man with a conscience," she wrote in *Biggie: Voletta Wallace Remembers Her Son* (2005). "He was a giver to anyone who asked. He was a man of his word. And he was loyal."

Voletta wrote in her book *Biggie* about her son's musical endeavors: "The noise was incredible. There was loud talking and then loud music, then loud talking and then banging on the furniture. I would say to myself, 'My God, what . . . is going on in my house?'" Voletta told Chris that she didn't think he could sing. "That is *not* music! That's noise," she recalled telling him in *Biggie.*

Finally Voletta banished Chris's music from the house, so her son started rehearsing in a friend's basement across the street. Soon Voletta noticed crowds gathering to hear her son's music. "I could not imagine," Voletta wrote in her book, "that Christopher was at the center of all that. It seemed that everyone on the block was gathering in a small basement just to hear him rap and do his 'music' thing."

Big Trouble for Big Chris

Chris's teachers and others who knew him were surprised when he started losing interest in his studies. Other kids had looked up to him; in high school, he had become a Big Brother so he could mentor troubled young people. "He worked well with kids, the younger ones. He didn't talk down to them," recalled Robert Izzo, as reported in *The Murder of Biggie Smalls.* Izzo was the coordinator of student affairs at Westinghouse High School in Brooklyn, where Chris was enrolled.

Still, Chris continued to cut classes. When he was in tenth grade, at age 17, he dropped out. "I knew he was never going back to school," Voletta later wrote. "We battled over this for three months. He cried and I cried. He cried and I cried some more. Then he stopped coming home."

Chris had fallen in with a tough crowd. In an interview with MTV, Chris said, "I was a full-time, one hundred-percent hustler. Sellin' drugs, wakin' up early in the morning, hittin' the set selling my [drugs] 'til the crack of dawn. My mother goin' to work would see me out there in the morning. That's how I was." However, according to the police in Brooklyn, Chris was never more than a small-time drug dealer—at the most, he made $5 or $10 on each sale. Although he was arrested several times, he was usually let go with warnings.

But when Chris visited some friends in North Carolina and was arrested for selling drugs, the police there were not willing to let him off. Chris's mother was forced to bail him out of jail by posting $25,000 **bond**—money she had received from a court settlement and that she had been saving for Chris's college education. When Chris returned from North Carolina, he promised his mother he would stop dealing drugs.

Groupies Already

Chris kept his word about staying away from drugs. He turned to music instead. After he had dropped out of school, he started spending a lot of time with his friend Chico Delvico, who loved rap as much as Chris did. Unlike Voletta Wallace, Chico's mother encouraged her son's talents, purchasing turntables and recording equipment for him. Chris and Chico spent a lot of time in Chico's room, trying out rhymes and beats. They made **demo tapes** to show their talents.

At the time, rap was going through an era of change. For years, many rap songs had an upbeat feel. Songs by such popular artists as DJ Jazzy Jeff and the Fresh Prince, MC Hammer, Kid 'N Play, and Sir Mix-A-Lot told playful stories of going to parties, dancing, meeting girls, driving expensive cars, and making narrow escapes from risky situations. At first, Chris Wallace mimicked their lighter style, but then he turned to a grittier hip-hop sound that was becoming known as gangsta rap. His rhymes took on a much darker tone, telling stories of robbery, murder, guns, and drugs. Using the name "Quest," Chris used Chico's bedroom **studio** to record several tapes of gangsta rap songs and gave them to a local record store to sell.

Chris soon developed a following in the neighborhood. Mister Cee, a Brooklyn-based rapper who saw Chris's potential, befriended the young rapper. He urged Chris to send a tape to the music magazine *The Source*, which reported on new talent in a column titled "Unsigned Hype." Mister Cee knew the column's writer, Matty C, and personally delivered the tape to the magazine. Matty C also was impressed with Chris's sound. In the March 1992 issue of *The Source*, Matty C reported that there was a new and exciting voice in gangsta rap music—a kid from Brooklyn who recorded under the name Quest. Matty C even ran Chris's picture with the column.

A Hypnotic Voice

Mister Cee had other important contacts in the rap world and used them to help launch Chris's career. Just as the March issue of *The Source* hit the newsstands, Mister Cee received a call from a young and ambitious executive who worked for Uptown Records. His name was

Sean Combs; in the music community, he was known as "Puffy." His job at Uptown was to recruit new talent.

Puffy Combs had worked with such hip-hop stars as Mary J. Blige, Heavy D, Father MC, and Jodeci. He knew gangsta rap was taking over the hip-hop scene, and he was eager to add gangsta acts to Uptown's stable of talent. Mister Cee told Combs that he had a demo tape from Quest, "this kid from the 'hood" who had not yet signed a contract with

People often gathered to hear Christopher Wallace perform his rhymes over the beats of popular songs. He soon began to collaborate with a friend, Chico Delvico, who had created a small recording studio in his mother's home.

Sean "Puffy" Combs was working as a talent scout for Uptown Records when he first heard Christopher Wallace's demo tape. He immediately recognized the young man's talent and signed him to a record contract with Uptown.

a record company. "He's big. He's hot," Mister Cee said, according to Scott. Combs told him to send Quest's tape.

Later, in an interview with MTV, Combs recalled the impact the tape made on him when he first played it. "As soon as I put it on, it just bugged me out," he said. "I listened to it for days and days, hours and hours." Chris's deep, husky voice seemed perfect for the nasty sound of gangsta rap. "His voice just hypnotized me," Combs recalled.

Combs hurried to track down Chris and offer him a recording contract. When Combs met Chris, he was stunned by his size. "How am I gonna market him?" Combs asked himself, according to Scott's biography. "He looks like a liquor-store robber."

Combs decided the name Quest would never do. He told Chris that since he was rapping about hard street life, he wanted him to adopt a gangsta's personality. He needed a new name—something that would tell fans not to mess with this big guy. Chris recalled seeing the movie *Let's Do it Again*, which includes a gangster character named Biggie Smalls. That name made Chris laugh, and it seemed perfect for the role he was about to adopt. From that point on, he planned to record under the name Biggie Smalls.

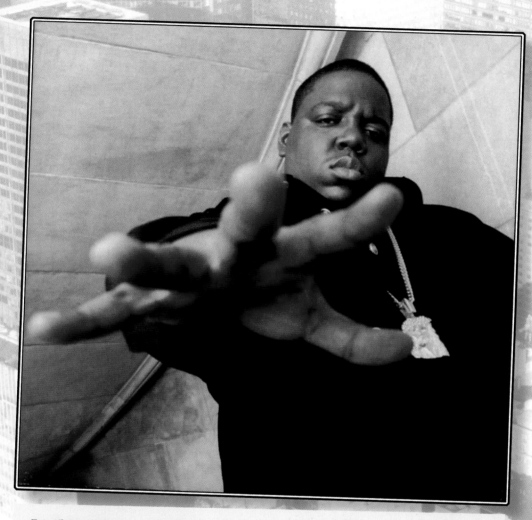

At the start of 1994, few people had heard of Biggie Smalls. By the end of the year, his situation had changed dramatically. The rapper became a major hip-hop star thanks to the success of his debut album.

3

The King of New York

Puffy Combs had great plans for his **protégé** Biggie, but wanted the young man to gain experience in a studio first. Combs hired him to provide background rhymes on a new Mary J. Blige album that Uptown Records was producing. Biggie did what Combs told him, but he was eager to release his own album and soon grew impatient.

"It seemed like everything took forever," Biggie later complained, according to Cheo Coker. "I was doing whatever I had to do, paying my dues with all the stuff they wanted me to do." Combs advised Biggie to be patient. The producer was still working out the details for Biggie's first album with Uptown.

Biggie had not yet started to record his songs when Combs had a falling out with Uptown executives in July 1993 and was fired from the label. However, Puffy Combs had become an influential figure in hip-hop music.

He had produced many successful albums for Uptown and seemed to possess a magic touch for turning unknown rappers into overnight celebrities. Combs decided he could build on this success by starting his own record label, which he named Bad Boy Entertainment. He decided to make Biggie Smalls Bad Boy's first big star. Combs and Biggie went to work in the studio and soon produced the album *Ready to Die*.

Released in 1994, the album featured seventeen tracks. Most of the songs glorified crime, murder, and gunfights. When asked why he gave the album such a morbid name, Biggie answered, according to Coker's book, "I'm just trying to say that I'm ready to die for this. . . . This is urgent. You got to be willing to do whatever you got to do to make this paper [money]."

Hip-hop critics proclaimed *Ready to Die* a true **anthem** of the streets. Biggie Smalls had found a way to channel the violence of urban life into rhymes that struck a chord with young blacks. *Ready to Die* would go on to sell more than four million copies and establish Biggie as a tremendous talent on the hip-hop scene. Two of the singles, "Big Poppa" and "One More Chance," each sold more than two million copies and reached the top ten on *Billboard* magazine's US Hot 100 chart.

Before Bad Boy released the album, Puffy Combs learned there was another rapper performing under the name Biggie Smalls and recording on a competing label. Lawyers for this other Biggie demanded that Combs find another name for his star. Combs and Wallace talked it over and came up with Notorious B.I.G.—a name that would appear on all of Wallace's albums. Still, Wallace preferred to be called Biggie. "Everybody knows who the real Smalls is," he insisted, according to Coker.

Gangsta Rap

The songs on *Ready to Die* tell dark, profanity-laced stories of murder, robbery, revenge, and abuse of women. Those are all the ingredients of gangsta rap, which portrays a harsh and ugly urban street life. According to Cathy Scott, in *The Murder of Biggie Smalls*, Biggie defended his choice of lyrics. He said,

"If I'd a worked at McDonald's, I'd a made rhyme about Big Macs and fries and stuff like that. I'm in Brooklyn, I see hustlin', I see killin', I see gamblin', I see girls, I see cars. That's what I rap about, what's in my environment."

The hard sound of gangsta rap had been growing in popularity since the late 1980s. At first, gangsta rap was performed mostly at clubs and on street corners because mainstream record companies refused to produce albums with such violent messages. Radio stations also hesitated to broadcast the songs because of the Federal Communications Commission's strict rules that prohibit profanity on the public airwaves. But by the late 1980s and early 1990s, gangsta rap had found a place in the public consciousness. One of the most influential early albums was

Notorious B.I.G. holds an award for his first album, *Ready to Die*. The record, released in 1994, was an immediate success. It contained several hit singles, sold more than four million copies, and was praised by many critics.

Straight Outta Compton (1989) by the rap group N.W.A, which told stories of the tough street life in the high-crime Southern California city of Compton. In 1992, Los Angeles-based rapper Ice-T gained national notoriety for his song "Cop Killer," which advocated shooting policemen. Although law-enforcement officials called for the song to be banned, the controversy helped sell records and make more people aware of gangsta rap.

Despite its continued popularity, gangsta rap has its critics. Before her death in 2005, one of the most vocal opponents of gangsta music was civil rights leader C. Delores Tucker. In 1995, Tucker's activism helped convince entertainment company Time Warner to stop producing gangsta rap albums. Tucker contended that gangsta rap is misogynistic, meaning it promotes hatred toward women. In a 1995 interview published in the *Buffalo News*, she said,

> **"I marched with the civil rights movement because I believed in it. I got involved with [the gangsta rap issue] to help bring to light something that is destroying our young black children. It's genocide. The lyrics promote profanity and misogyny. It glamorizes drug use, rape, and violence. Children are able to purchase this pornographic filth and that has to stop."**

Although Tucker's efforts did focus public concern on the dangerous messages in gangsta rap music, fans continued to support the music. Throughout the 1990s, the hip-hop careers of gangsta stars continued to flourish, and no one's career seemed to be skyrocketing more than Biggie's.

Success Brings Problems

Having released his first album, Biggie needed to spend a lot of time on tour. He appeared in concerts and performed at clubs to promote *Ready to Die*. Throughout his travels, he was accompanied by a group of teenage backup singers that he had organized back in Brooklyn and called the Junior M.A.F.I.A. Among the singers he recruited for the group was Kimberly Jones, who would eventually find fame in her own right as rap star Lil' Kim. Soon Biggie helped produce the Junior M.A.F.I.A.'s album *Conspiracy* (1995), as well as solo albums by Lil' Kim.

Biggie helped to organize the group Junior M.A.F.I.A., and produced their first album in 1995. Lil' Kim, a member of the Junior M.A.F.I.A., developed a close relationship with Biggie. He produced her solo debut album, *Hard Core*, in 1996.

Biggie's life on the road was often exciting, but it could also be hectic and disappointing. Although Biggie was a major rap star, his concerts were not always well promoted. As a result, he would sometimes arrive at an auditorium to discover a very small crowd. When this happened, Biggie worried that his career as a rap star was fading. "I did five venues where there were like thirteen people in 'em," he once complained, Coker's book reported. "My boys were telling me it was the promoters not doing their jobs, but I was slowly but surely thinking it was over."

Biggie's doubts were always erased, though, when his bus would roll into another city and find an enthusiastic crowd waiting for him to perform. During this period, the fans started calling him Big Poppa, after the hit song from the *Ready to Die* album. Often fans would crowd the lobbies of the hotels where he stayed while on tour. A member of the Junior M.A.F.I.A., DJ Enuff, told Coker, "He was the Don, he was the leader. We just had to respect that."

His success as a hip-hop star earned Biggie yet another nickname: the King of New York. Biggie borrowed the nickname from a 1990 movie in which the crime boss, a character named Frank White, takes this nickname. The boss has money and power and therefore feels he is rightfully the "king." On *Ready to Die*, Biggie referred to himself as "the black Frank White."

Biggie certainly had money—*Ready to Die* earned him millions of dollars. He also had power in the hip-hop world. As Bad Boy's biggest star, he commanded as much as $65,000 a show to perform. Also, his promotion of the Junior M.A.F.I.A. and Lil' Kim showed he had an eye for other rap talent.

But Biggie also started living the lifestyle he portrayed in his music. In 1995 he was arrested for assault after attacking a record promoter in Camden, New Jersey—an incident that put him in jail for four days. In the same year, Biggie was convicted of assaulting fans outside a Manhattan nightclub. In 1996, police raided his home in Teaneck, New Jersey, where they found marijuana and several dangerous weapons, including handguns, a submachine gun, and hollow-point bullets. Also in 1996, he was charged with drug possession after police found him smoking marijuana while sitting in his car on a Brooklyn street. "I'd rather be dead than in jail," Biggie said, according to Coker, shortly after his release from jail because of the Camden incident.

Despite his success, Biggie could not avoid problems with the law. In March 1996 he was arrested in Manhattan after using a baseball bat to attack two fans who had asked for his autograph outside a nightclub.

In 1995, Biggie married singer Faith Evans, and in October 1996, their son C.J. was born. In this 2005 photo, eight-year-old C.J., looking much like his father, arrives with his mother at an event sponsored by the music channel VH1.

Changing His Lifestyle

With the possibility of a longer jail term hanging over him, and sensing this was no way to live, Biggie tried to change his life. He took long walks around his old Brooklyn neighborhood, seeking out young people who seemed to be aimless and encouraging them to go back to school. If he found a teenager selling drugs, he would give the teen money in exchange for giving up the drug business.

Biggie also became more interested in family life. He already had a daughter, T'yanna Wallace, who had been born to his girlfriend Jan Jackson in August 1993. However, he and Jan had split up five months after the baby's birth. In 1995 Biggie met Faith Evans, a rhythm and blues singer who recorded on Combs's label. Just eight days after they met, Biggie and Faith married. Soon they became the parents of a baby boy, C.J. Their marriage was often strained—Biggie blamed their troubles on their lightning-fast courtship—and they eventually separated. Still, Biggie said fatherhood had made him a more responsible person. "I want to see my kids get old," he told *Vibe* magazine. "I want to go to my daughter's wedding. I want to go to my son's wedding. I want to go to their sons' weddings."

Meanwhile, he returned to the studio. Biggie's second album, which would be titled *Life After Death*, contained a strong gangsta flavor, but it also showed that Biggie had a new outlook on life. In the songs "Sky Is the Limit" and "Miss U," Biggie raps about his love for his children and his interest in watching them grow up.

Still, there is a dark mood to *Life After Death*. For the album's advertisements, Puffy Combs had Biggie photographed dressed in black, leaning against a tombstone in a graveyard while his ghost hovers nearby. And the cover of the album would show Biggie dressed like an **undertaker** in a tall black hat and long overcoat, leaning against the back of a black **hearse**. Those images, it would turn out, said a lot about his future.

Sean Combs and Suge Knight ignore each other on a sidewalk in Beverly Hills. By mid-1996, it seemed likely that the war of words between Bad Boy Entertainment and Death Row Records would soon take a violent and tragic turn.

4

The Rap War

Puffy Combs and Suge Knight had climbed to the top of the hip-hop world by vastly different paths. Both had been born into harsh environments, but had succeeded in building music empires. Yet the escalating rivalry between the two men and their music labels made a fatal collision between their biggest stars seem unavoidable.

Sean Combs had been born in Harlem, the depressed and mostly African-American neighborhood of New York. His father was a drug dealer who was shot to death when Sean was three years old. His mother, Janice Combs, aimed to make a better life for her children and struggled to raise them in a crime-free environment. When Sean was eleven years old, Janice managed to move her family to a better neighborhood in suburban Mount Vernon, New York.

Combs was intelligent and hardworking. Following high school, he enrolled at Howard University in Washington, where he majored in business administration. As a college **sophomore**, he won an **internship** at Uptown Records. Combs proved to be so valuable to Uptown that he soon dropped out of college to accept a full-time job with the label, which assigned him the task of bringing in new talent. He had already discovered Jodeci and Mary J. Blige, before checking out young rapper Christopher Wallace.

An Intimidator

Like Combs, Suge Knight found a way to rise above a childhood of poverty. But unlike Combs, who used his intelligence and business **savvy** to succeed, Knight fought his way to the top of the rap world with threats and intimidation and by simply being tougher than the next guy.

Born in Compton, Knight had grown into a large, athletic man. Knight played college football and briefly had a pro career, but he gave up football to work as a bodyguard for R&B singer Bobby Brown. That experience introduced Knight to the music world, where he made important contacts. At first, he promoted rap concerts and became friendly with the rap producer and artist Dr. Dre. In 1990, he moved deeper into the world of hip-hop music by joining with Dr. Dre to form his own record label. He quickly surrounded himself with thugs. "We called it Death Row 'cause most everybody had been involved with the law," he is quoted as saying in *The Killing of Tupac Shakur*. "A majority of our people was parolees or incarcerated. It's no joke."

Knight had many run-ins with the law, starting in 1987 when he allegedly shot a man outside his Las Vegas apartment, then stole the victim's car. Knight pleaded guilty and was placed on **probation** for three years—meaning he did not have to serve jail time but was required to maintain good behavior and check in regularly with law enforcement officers. Three years later, he was charged with breaking a man's jaw and holding a gun to his face. Again he was placed on probation. Meanwhile, he is said to have maintained close contact with a notorious Compton street gang known as the Bloods. He drove red cars, wore red suits, and even had the walls of his swimming pool painted red—an obvious show of allegiance to these gang members, because red was the Bloods' color.

Growing Tension

While Combs and Knight had agreed to meet at Quincy Jones's 1995 rap summit to discuss their differences, the meeting did little to settle

Suge Knight's Death Row Records became a major label with the success of Dr. Dre's 1992 album *The Chronic*, a hip-hop classic that helped launch the career of Snoop Dogg. However, Knight's heavy-handed methods often got him into trouble with the law.

Biggie speaks at the 1996 Soul Train Music Awards in Los Angeles. According to newspaper reporters, Biggie and Tupac confronted each other while backstage at the show. However, the two rappers denied the incident occurred.

the simmering East Coast–West Coast Rap War. A few weeks after the summit, the dispute between Death Row and Bad Boy stopped being primarily a war of words and became much more serious.

The Bad Boy rappers continued seething about the comments Knight had made about Combs at *The Source* awards. On September 24, 1995, that anger took a violent turn. On that night, Combs and Biggie attended a party in Atlanta thrown by Jermaine Dupri, the founder of So So Def Records. Knight also attended the party, along with a large contingent from Death Row. Soon the tensions between the East Coast and West Coast rappers surfaced. One of Combs's body-guards, Anthony "Wolf" Jones, exchanged angry words with Jake "The Violator" Robles, a member of the Bloods gang and a close associate of Knight's. Suddenly shots were fired. A bullet hit Robles, and he died a week later. Knight blamed Combs, claiming he had ordered the Robles shooting.

A few months later, Biggie Smalls was drawn into the center of the war. On March 29, 1996, Biggie performed at the *Soul Train* Music Awards. Many Death Row rappers were in attendance, including Tupac Shakur, Dr. Dre, and Snoop Dogg.

Although Biggie had once been friends with Tupac, in November 1994 that friendship had been destroyed. That was when Shakur was shot five times while entering a New York City recording studio. Biggie had been recording a song in the studio when Shakur was shot. He called for an ambulance, and visited Shakur in the hospital the next day. Shakur survived the attack, but came to believe that Biggie had somehow been involved in the shooting.

Biggie vigorously denied he had anything to do with the attack. However, Shakur interpreted the lyrics of Notorious B.I.G.'s 1995 single "Who Shot Ya?" as bragging that he had been behind the attack. Shakur responded with the single "Hit 'Em Up," in which he vengefully boasted of seducing Biggie's wife, Faith Evans. When *Vibe* magazine asked Biggie how he felt about the insult, the star responded that he wouldn't perpetuate a fight:

> **❝It hurt but I kinda look at it like business. When you at the top, you gotta go for the top person's neck, you know what I'm sayin'? You just gotta get your spot, you know what I'm sayin'? That's what he wanted. I can't be mad at him for that. He just doin' what he gotta do. I couldn't be the one to do it back, though— that's not my style.❞**

Despite these words, the feud had now become very personal for both of the rappers. At the 1996 *Soul Train* awards, Biggie encountered Shakur backstage. The two exchanged angry words. Newspapers reported that Shakur threatened Biggie with a gun, but both men denied that happened.

An injured Tupac Shakur is wheeled into a New York courthouse, December 1, 1994. A day earlier, the rapper had been shot five times while entering a recording studio. Shakur became convinced that Biggie had set up the shooting, although Biggie denied any involvement.

Shakur's Murder

Less than six months later, on September 7, 1996, Tupac Shakur was shot. That night Shakur and Knight had attended a heavyweight fight at a casino-hotel in Las Vegas. While leaving, they got into a scuffle with Orlando Anderson, a member of the Crips—another Compton street

Tupac was gunned down in Las Vegas on September 7, 1996, and died six days later. Some people suspected Biggie was involved in the murder because of their feud. Biggie and his friends claimed he was at home in New Jersey when the shooting occurred.

gang that has long feuded with the Bloods. After beating Anderson, Shakur and Knight headed for a party at a Las Vegas nightclub. Knight drove. When he stopped at a traffic light, another vehicle pulled alongside his car. Shots were fired into Knight's car. Knight was wounded slightly when a piece of flying glass hit him in the back of the neck, but Shakur was fatally wounded. Suspicion immediately fell on Biggie, but he denied that he had anything to do with the murder. Biggie claimed he had been home in New Jersey the night Shakur was shot.

If Biggie was worried about his own safety, he didn't let his friends or fans know. Although he continued to travel with bodyguards, Biggie still maintained a busy schedule. There was work to be done to complete his second album, *Life After Death*, as well as dates to keep for live performances.

On the night of March 9, 1997, Biggie's schedule took him to Los Angeles, where he presented an award at the *Soul Train* Music Awards. Because the awards show was held on the West Coast, the audience was made up mostly of West Coast rap fans. As Biggie walked onto the stage, he was greeted with boos and jeers. He tried to ignore the anger. Ironically, the biggest award that night went to Shakur, whose 1996 album *All Eyez on Me* won the award for Best Rap Album.

Following the awards show, Biggie attended a party at the Peterson Automotive Museum in Los Angeles. Every rap star in town seemed to be at the party. In addition to Biggie, other rappers who attended the party were Busta Rhymes, Da Brat, and Yo-Yo. The actor Wesley Snipes and comedian Chris Tucker were also in the crowd. Puffy Combs attended as well. As for Biggie, he was thoroughly enjoying himself. Although he had a leg injury that slowed him down, he sat at a table just off the dance floor and fans constantly made their way to the table, where he joked with them and signed autographs.

More than two thousand people crowded into the museum. Just after midnight, the fire marshal announced that there were too many people in the building, which could result in a catastrophe if a fire broke out. He ordered everyone to leave.

Puffy's Prayers

Biggie left the building and climbed into the passenger seat of a car that was to take him to another party. His driver got behind the wheel. Two friends, Lil' Cease and D-Roc Butler, sat in the back seats of the vehicle.

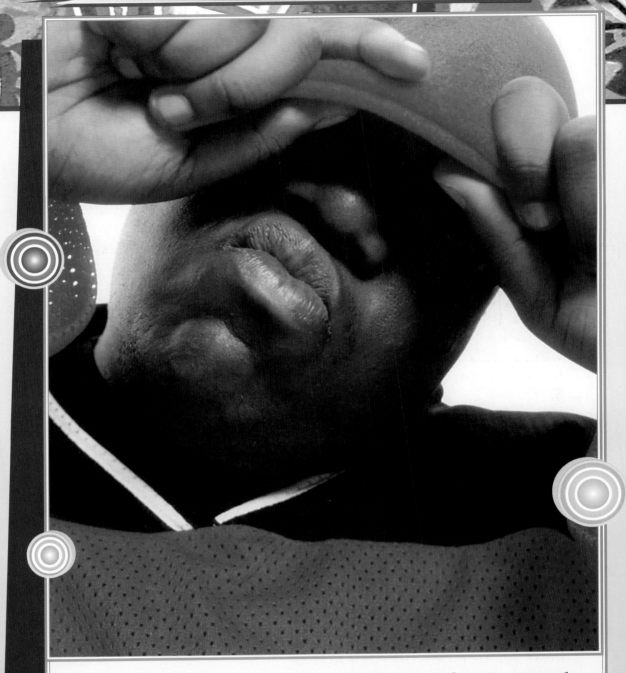

This publicity photo of Notorious B.I.G. was taken to promote the rapper's second album, *Life After Death*. Biggie was proud of the way the album had turned out, but would not live to see it released.

Biggie started playing a tape of *Life After Death*, which was scheduled for release in two weeks.

The car left for the party. Behind it followed two other cars carrying Combs and others from Bad Boy. The convoy didn't get very far

Bullet holes are visible in the door of the GMC Suburban in which Biggie Smalls was riding the night he was murdered. The rapper was gunned down after leaving a party in Los Angeles early in the morning of March 9, 1997.

though. Just one hundred yards from the museum, Biggie's driver stopped at a red light. While he was waiting at the intersection, a black car pulled alongside. Suddenly, a man in the car extended his hand outside the window. He held a gun and fired seven shots into Biggie's car. Biggie was hit all seven times and slumped over in his seat. He was the only one in the car hit by the gunfire.

The car with the gunman zoomed away. Puffy Combs was still in the car behind Biggie's. "I jumped out of my car and ran over to his," Combs later told the *New York Daily News*. "I was saying the Lord's Prayer and Hail Marys. I was begging God to help him out. I was touching him and talking to him in his ear."

Puffy's prayers were not enough. One hour after Biggie was shot, the 24-year-old rapper was pronounced dead at a Los Angeles hospital.

HIP-HOP ON A HIGHER LEVEL

XXL

IN STEREO

1NCE AGAIN BABY-BABY!

GETO BOYS REUNION
50 CENT'S TRIUMPH
FIELD MOB
RAEKWON

THE MAKING OF
LIFE AFTER DEATH

STARRING
P. DIDDY
LIL' KIM
D-DOT
DJ PREMIER
BONE THUGS -N-HARMONY
RZA
LIL' CEASE
JADAKISS
DMC

BIGGIE SMALLS • 1972-1997 • R.I.P.

NOTORIOUS B.I.G.
THE LOST TAPES

XXclusive never-before-seen interview with The King of New York

In the years since his death, Notorious B.I.G. has remained very popular among hip-hop fans. He has sold millions of albums and continued to be featured in hip-hop publications such as this issue of *XXL* magazine from April 2003.

5

His Spirit Lives On

Thousands of hip-hop fans lined the streets as the funeral procession carrying Biggie's body made its way through Clinton Hill. When the procession stopped briefly by Biggie's old home, the mourners saw two little girls holding a sign. According to *The Murder of Biggie Smalls*, the sign read, "We love you Biggie. Save our youth. Stop the violence."

Among the mourners who attended Biggie's funeral were rap's biggest stars, including Foxy Brown, DJ Kool Herc, Queen Latifah, Mary J. Blige, Dr. Dre, Sister Souljah, and Busta Rhymes. Members of the Junior M.A.F.I.A., including Lil' Kim, also attended the funeral, paying their respects to the rap star who had helped launch their careers. Puffy Combs delivered the **eulogy**, and Biggie's widow, Faith Evans, sang the gospel song "Walk With Me, Lord."

Reporters mingled among members of the crowd who were watching the procession pass. The reporters asked people how the rap star, who had recorded a mere two albums, could generate such an emotional response from thousands of people. One mourner, Carol Williams of Brooklyn, told *People* magazine that the response from Biggie's fans reminded her of the outpouring of grief that Americans had shown shortly after the assassination of President John F. Kennedy in 1963. She said, "They're here to express love. It's like when John F. Kennedy passed on. Biggie may not have been presidential material, but to the extent that he was able to come from this way of life and succeed, he means a lot to people."

"More than a Rapper"

Life After Death, released two weeks after Biggie died, immediately shot to the top of the hip-hop charts. The double album received critical praise from many reviewers. Nearly 700,000 copies of *Life After Death* were sold in the first week; eventually more than 5 million copies were sold, making *Life After Death* one of the best-selling rap albums of all time.

As with *Ready to Die*, Biggie's second album contains gritty stories of life on the streets. Songs from *Life After Death* like "Somebody's Gotta Die" and "You're Nobody ('Til Somebody Kills You)" made some fans wonder if Biggie had predicted his death. Overall, however, the album has a more commercial sound than *Ready to Die*. The single "Mo Money Mo Problems" was a crossover hit, rising to number 22 on Billboard's Top 40 chart. Both "Mo Money Mo Problems" and "Hypnotize" hit number one on the Hot Rap Singles chart, while "Going Back to Cali" reached number three.

Following *Life After Death*, Bad Boy produced two **posthumous** albums of Biggie's music: *Born Again* (1999), and *Duets: The Final Chapter* (2005). *Born Again* includes some tracks that Biggie recorded before his death; to fill out the album, Combs invited some other rappers, including Busta Rhymes, Snoop Dogg, Redman, Method Man, and Eminem, to contribute to the unfinished songs. *Duets: The Final Chapter* features some of Biggie's old tracks laid over new beats while other rappers add their voices. Some critics complained that neither album measured up to the work Biggie had produced while he was alive. Nevertheless, the two albums have proven to be popular among Biggie's fans.

Biggie was mourned by tens of thousands of fans. Many gathered on the streets of New York to observe his funeral procession on March 18, 1997. This photo was taken in the Bedford-Stuyvesant neighborhood of Brooklyn.

Shortly after the release of *Duets: The Final Chapter*, Combs told *The Source* magazine, "Biggie was the greatest rapper of all time. [His death] left a huge void in music, Hip-Hop and our culture. He was more than a rapper, he was more than a personality; he was a visionary."

A group of Biggie's friends and family members accept an award on his behalf at the MTV Video Music Awards ceremony in September 1997. Biggie's song "Hypnotize," one of several hit singles from *Life After Death*, was named Best Rap Video.

The Investigation Continues

Police have never solved the murders of Tupac Shakur and Notorious B.I.G., although accusations have surfaced. Former Los Angeles police detective Russell Poole, who investigated Biggie's murder, as well as journalist Randall Sullivan, believe the murders were committed by **rogue** Los Angeles police officers. In stories published in *Rolling Stone* in June 2001 and December 2005, Sullivan quotes sources who said the rogue cops were on the payroll of Suge Knight. According to Sullivan's stories, Knight had the cops kill Shakur because Shakur owed him $3 million and didn't want to pay, and Knight had the men kill Biggie to eliminate the top Bad Boy recording artist.

Knight has denied the charges, but in 2001 Biggie's mother and his widow filed a **lawsuit** against the Los Angeles police, alleging that members of the department assisted Knight in the murder of Biggie. The lawsuit came to trial in 2005. However, U.S. District Judge Florence-Marie Cooper declared a mistrial when she learned that the Los Angeles police had withheld important evidence from the attorneys for Voletta Wallace and Faith Evans. In January 2006, the judge ordered the city of Los Angeles to pay more than $1 million to Biggie's family because the police had withheld evidence.

Cooper's ruling indicates that the judge believes there is much that remains hidden about Biggie's murder and possibly Shakur's as well. Biggie's family plans to refile the lawsuit. Perry Sanders, an attorney for Voletta Wallace, told the *New York Times*, "We intend to uncover the real truth."

Knight has denied that he was involved in the two murders. Actually, he was in prison when Biggie was shot. At the time of Shakur's murder, Knight was on probation after pleading guilty to assaulting two rap singers in a Los Angeles recording studio. Because he had participated in the assault on Orlando Anderson in the lobby of the MGM Grand after the heavyweight fight, he was found to be in violation of his probation. California Judge J. Stephen Czuleger sentenced him to a prison term of nine years. Knight told Judge Czuleger that he was trying to break up the fight between Tupac and Anderson in order to save Anderson from a further beating, but the judge refused to buy the story.

Suge Knight ran his rap empire from a cell at Mule Creek State Prison in Ione, California. He behaved during his time there, and after five years earned a **parole**. Knight's record label has continued to have problems, though. Snoop Dogg and Dr. Dre left Death Row to pursue careers elsewhere, and the label has never regained its former prominence. In recent years, Knight has found it difficult to shake his image as a thug. In 2004, friends of Knight scuffled with two rappers at a *Vibe* magazine awards show. And in 2005, Knight was shot in the leg during an altercation at a party hosted by rapper Kanye West.

As for Combs, who now calls himself Diddy, he has continued to produce hip-hop albums. He has branched out into other directions also, producing clothing and cosmetic lines, and has headed television and film projects. In 2001, critics praised his acting when he appeared as a condemned prisoner in the film *Monster's Ball.*

New Accusations

While Knight and Combs lived on and kept producing rap music, the unsolved murders of Tupac and Biggie kept the stars' families, fans, and others unsettled. In 2002, the *Los Angeles Times* published its own findings about Tupac's death. In a series of stories, it alleged that Biggie paid $1 million to Crips member Orlando Anderson to kill Tupac Shakur, and that Biggie even supplied Anderson with the gun. By the time these articles were published, neither Biggie nor Anderson were around to tell their sides of the story. Anderson also had been shot to death; he had died in a gang shootout unrelated to the East Coast–West Coast Rap War.

Until his death, Biggie claimed that he had been at his New Jersey home the night of Shakur's murder. The newspaper reported, though, that Biggie had spent that night in the MGM Grand under an assumed name and that he had summoned Anderson and other Crips to his suite to arrange Shakur's murder. When they agreed to slay the Death Row rapper, the newspaper reported, Biggie handed the gang members a gun and instructed them to use it in the slaying. According to the *Times* report, Biggie said he wanted the satisfaction of knowing that the bullet that would kill Shakur had come from his gun.

One *Los Angeles Times* story said that after the assault on Anderson in the hotel lobby, Anderson and the other Crips followed Shakur and Knight and caught up to them before they reached the party they planned to attend. Anderson fired the fatal shots, the newspaper reported.

The *Los Angeles Times* stories provoked a bitter reaction from Voletta Wallace and other members of Biggie's family. A statement that Wallace family members released said in part:

❝We are outraged at the false and damaging statements made in the *Los Angeles Times* . . . regarding Christopher (the Notorious B.I.G.'s) Wallace's alleged involvement in Tupac Shakur's death. . . .

Biggie's widow, Faith Evans, leaves a Los Angeles courtroom, July 2005. Evans and Voletta Wallace filed a lawsuit against the Los Angeles Police Department, alleging that renegade members of the department had been involved in Biggie's murder.

For the record, Christopher (the Notorious B.I.G.) Wallace was at home in New Jersey on the night of Tupac Shakur's murder, with friends who will continue to testify for his whereabouts since he is unable to defend himself. . . .

Christopher (the Notorious B.I.G.) Wallace's friends and family will continue to stand by him and support

Voletta Wallace continues to seek her son's killer. "All I want, all I ever wanted is justice for my son's death," she told the website allhiphop.com. "All I ever wanted was the truth. And that's not asking too much."

his memory in the face of this latest accusation against his character and his life.

This false story is a disrespect to not only our family but the family of Tupac Shakur. Both men will have no peace as long as stories such as these continue to be written."

Biggie's Vision

In the years since her son's death, Voletta Wallace has used money from Biggie's estate to establish the Christopher Wallace Memorial Foundation, which provides money for literacy programs at inner city schools as well as for other programs to help urban youth. Recalls Voletta Wallace in her book about Biggie,

"My son was up and coming faster than anyone else in the rap world. He, for the first time that I recall, actually was serious about something. He had a vision for himself with his music career. He was not looking to be involved with any rivalry.

He had a mantra: negativity brings failure. . . . That's where Christopher's head was. He wasn't interested in being in the middle of a feud or a rap war. He wanted to be successful. My son had something to live for. . . .

Christopher had big, big dreams. He had a plan. He had a grand vision."

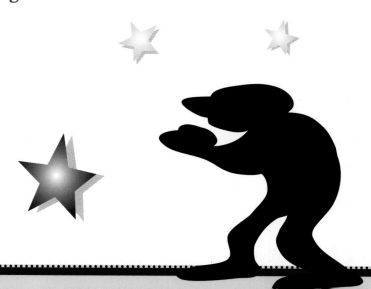

1972 Christopher Wallace is born on May 21 in the Clinton Hill neighborhood of Brooklyn, New York.

1989 Wallace drops out of school and becomes a small-time drug dealer.

1992 Wallace sends a demo tape to *The Source* magazine, which features him as a dynamic new talent on the hip-hop scene; Sean "Puffy" Combs signs Wallace to a contract with Uptown Records.

1993 Combs leaves Uptown Records and forms Bad Boy Entertainment; he signs Wallace to a recording contract under the name Biggie Smalls.

1994 *Ready to Die* is released under Biggie's new name, Notorious B.I.G. In November, rival rapper Tupac Shakur is shot as he enters the lobby of a New York recording studio. Shakur accuses Biggie of planning the assault, touching off the East Coast–West Coast Rap War.

1995 Biggie and *Ready to Die* win four awards at *The Source* magazine's Second Annual Hip-Hop Awards. Biggie is arrested for assault in cases in New York City and Camden, New Jersey. Biggie meets and marries rhythm and blues singer Faith Evans. In September, Death Row Records founder Suge Knight blames Combs for planning the murder of his associate, Jake "The Violator" Robles.

1996 A police raid on Biggie's home in Teaneck, New Jersey, uncovers guns and ammunition; Biggie is also charged with smoking marijuana in a car on a Brooklyn street. On September 7, Shakur is murdered in Las Vegas, Nevada.

1997 Biggie Smalls is murdered on March 9 after leaving a party in Los Angeles; his album *Life After Death* is released two weeks later.

1999 The album *Born Again* is released.

2001 Voletta Wallace and Faith Evans file a lawsuit against the Los Angeles police, alleging that members of the department assisted Suge Knight in the murder of Biggie.

2002 The *Los Angeles Times* publishes a series of stories alleging that Biggie paid $1 million to Crips member Orlando Anderson to kill Tupac Shakur.

2005 *Duets: The Final Chapter* is released; in June, the Wallace-Evans lawsuit comes to trial, but it is dismissed when U.S. District Judge Florence-Marie Cooper rules that the Los Angeles police withheld evidence from Biggie's mother and widow.

2006 Judge Cooper fines the Los Angeles police $1 million for withholding evidence.

Albums

1994 *Ready to Die*
1997 *Life After Death*
1999 *Born Again*
2005 *Duets: The Final Chapter*

Awards and Recognition

1995 Winner, *The Source* magazine's Hip-Hop Music Awards for New Artist of the Year, Lyricist of the Year, and Live Performer of the Year, and for *Ready to Die*, Album of the Year.

Winner, *Billboard* Music Awards for Rap Artist of the Year, while Biggie's single, "One More Chance," named Rap Single of the Year.

1996 Nominated for a Grammy Award for Best Rap Solo Performance for "Big Poppa."

1997 Winner of an MTV Video Music Award for Best Rap Video for "Hypnotize."

Spin magazine names Biggie Artist of the Year.

1998 Nominated for three Grammy Awards for Best Rap Solo Performance for "Hypnotize," Best Rap Performance by a Duo or Group with Mase and Puff Daddy for "Mo Money Mo Problems," and Best Rap Album for *Life After Death*.

Winner of a *Soul Train* Music Award for Best Rhythm and Blues/Soul Album, Male for *Life After Death* and with Mase and Puff Daddy, Best Rhythm and Blues/Soul Album and Best Rhythm and Blues/Soul or Rap Music Video for "Mo Money Mo Problems."

Nominated for an MTV Video Music Award for Best Rap Video for "Mo Money Mo Problems" with Mase and Puff Daddy.

1999 "Mo Money Mo Problems," selected 23rd on the list of MTV's 100 Greatest Videos Ever Made.

2001 *The Source* names Biggie Smalls Greatest MC of All Time.

2003 Selected by VH1 as fourth on the list of 50 Greatest Hip Hop Artists.

"Mo Money Mo Problems" selected 58th on the list of VH1's 100 Best Songs of the Past 25 Years.

Ready to Die selected 133rd and *Life After Death* selected 483rd on the list of the 500 Greatest Albums of All Time by *Rolling Stone*.

Books

Coker, Cheo Hodari. *Unbelievable: The Life, Death, and Afterlife of the Notorious B.I.G.* New York: Three Rivers Press, 2003.

Scott, Cathy. *The Killing of Tupac Shakur.* Las Vegas, Nev.: Huntington Press, 2002.

————. *The Murder of Biggie Smalls.* New York: St. Martin's Press, 2000.

Sullivan, Randall. *LAbyrinth: A Detective Investigates the Murders of Tupac Shakur and Notorious B.I.G.* New York: Atlantic Monthly Press, 2002.

Wallace, Voletta, and Tremell McKenzie. *Biggie: Voletta Wallace Remembers Her Son, Christopher Wallace, AKA Notorious B.I.G.* New York: Atria Books, 2005.

Periodicals

Anderson, Tomika. "Long Kiss Good Night." *The Source* no. 195 (January 2006): p. 81.

Farley, Christopher John. "From the Driver's Side: Gangsta-Rap Mogul 'Suge' Knight Finally Breaks His Silence on Tupac Shakur's Unsolved Murder." *Time* vol. 148, no. 16 (September 30, 1996): p. 70.

Hunter, Karen. "Civil Rights Activist Turns Her Attention to Turning Down the Hate in Rap Lyrics." *Buffalo News* (August 22, 1995): p. C-5.

Leeds, Jeff. "Mistrial Adds New Mystery to the Death of a Rap Star." *New York Times* (July 9, 2005): p. B-7.

Philips, Chuck. "Who Killed Tupac Shakur?" *Chicago Tribune* (September 6, 2002). Available at www.chicagotribune.com/la-fi-tupac6sep06,0,3670705.story.

Philips, Chuck, and Andrew Blankstein. "Judge Chides L.A. in Rapper Killing." *Los Angeles Times* (January 21, 2006). Available at www.latimes.com/news/local/los_angeles_metro/la-me-biggie21jan21,0,7901437.story?coll=la-commun-los_angeles-metro.

Sullivan, Randall. "The Murder of the Notorious B.I.G." *Rolling Stone* (June 7, 2001): p. 80.

————. "The Unsolved Mystery of the Notorious B.I.G.: The Murder. The Cover-up. The Conspiracy." *Rolling Stone* (December 15, 2005): p. 124.

Web Sites

http://www.badboyonline.com

The Internet site for Bad Boy Entertainment includes a history of the company founded by Sean Combs as well as news about Bad Boy rappers and their latest releases.

http://foia.fbi.gov/foiaindex/cripsbloods.htm

Maintained by the Federal Bureau of Investigation, this site has an extensive archive of newspaper and magazine stories on the Crips and Bloods. A study on the gangs compiled by researchers at the University of the Pacific McGeorge School of Law can also be downloaded from the site.

http://www.mtv.com/music/#/music/artist/notorious_big/bio.jhtml

MTV has established this Web site tracing the career of Notorious B.I.G.; it highlights his contributions to music as well as his involvement in the East Coast–West Coast Rap War.

http://www.faithevansonline.com

Official Web site of Biggie's widow, rhythm and blues singer Faith Evans.

http://www.pbs.org/wgbh/pages/frontline/shows/lapd/bare.html

Companion Web site to the PBS *Frontline* documentary "LAPD Blues," which traces the scandal involving corrupt Los Angeles police officers, including those suspected of involvement in the murders of Notorious B.I.G. and Tupac Shakur.

anthem—a song that provides a powerful message for a social movement.

bond—cash posted to release from prison someone charged with a crime; the money guarantees the person charged will appear for trial.

demo tape—a recording made to give music producers and others an idea of how a new song might sound. These are often made on simple recording equipment with minimal instrumentation.

eulogy—words spoken during a funeral praising the deceased person; usually delivered by a close friend or family member.

hearse—large vehicle used to transport a dead person.

internship—period in which a college student receives on-the-job training.

lawsuit—document filed in a civil court by people who believe their rights have been violated by others; if successful, the people who have filed the case are often awarded money payable by the guilty parties.

parole—status granted to a prisoner that permits him or her to leave jail before his or her entire sentence has been served.

posthumous—issued or released after the death of the artist or creator.

probation—status granted to a criminal defendant that permits him or her to serve a sentence outside jail.

protégé—young person trained in his or her career by an older and experienced person.

rogue—dishonest person, often working secretly for evil purposes.

savvy—intelligence, especially in relation to business or politics.

sophomore—student in the second year of high school or college.

studio—place established for an artist to work, usually featuring the tools and equipment necessary to perform the artist's work, such as recording music.

summit—meeting scheduled to resolve differences and find common ground among enemies.

undertaker—professional who oversees all matters relating to a funeral and who often prepares the body for burial or cremation.

urban—relating to a city.

Hal Marcovitz is a journalist who has written more than 70 books for young readers as well as the satirical novel *Painting the White House.* He lives in Chalfont, Pennsylvania, with his wife Gail and daughters Ashley and Michelle.

Picture Credits

page

 2: Everrett Collection
 8: AP Photo/Mark Lennihan
11: NMI/Death Row Records
12: Everrett Collection
14: Photofest
17: Zuma Press/Nancy Kaszerman
18: PRNewsFoto/NMI
21: Photofest
22: KRT/Charles Trainor Jr.
24: Bad Boy Entertainment/NMI
27: Miramax/Photofest
29: PRNewsFoto/NMI
31: AP Photo/Adam Nadel

32: Fashion Wire Daily/Ali Goldstein
34: Splash News
37: KRT/Giulio Marcocchi
38: Reuters/Fred Prouser
40: KRT/David Hanschuh
41: AFP/Death Row Records
43: KRT/Bad Boy Entertainment
44: Zuma Press/Mike Meadows
46: NMI/Michelle Feng
49: KRT
50: AP Photo/Adam Nadel
53: Reuters/Mario Anzuoni
54: UPI Photo/Jim Ruymen

Front cover: Zuma Press/Jane Caine
Back cover: KRT/Bad Boy Entertainment